The Faith Walk

Nyesha Greer

Dedication

This book is dedicated to my children Eli and Ali Greer. My greatest desire is not to give you the world but to give you Jesus. May this book be a blessing to you as you grow your faith in the Lord. I love you always.

- Mom

Contents

Prologue	9
God is the Truth	11
What to Expect When You are Expecting	13
The Wilderness	16
Renewing Your Mind	21
Patience in Faith	25
Faith is a Weapon	27
Overflowing Faith	29
Take Time to Build	33
Respond in Faith	35
Manna for the Moment	39
Provision is Always Now	41
Growing your Faith	45
What Do You See	47
Laser-Focused Faith	51
God is Thinking About You	55
Give God Your Desires	57
More Than a Journey	61

Prologue

And now faith is the substance of things hoped for and the evidence of things not seen (Hebrews 11:1, KJV).

What is faith? Faith has been preached by many anointed men and women of God, each providing their revelation of what the Holy Spirit has shown them. Hebrews 11:1 states, "Now faith is the substance of things hoped for and the evidence of things not seen." We use this faith to hope for the things we cannot see. Faith is not as complicated as it sounds. Faith is acting like God is telling the truth. Seems all too simple to assume such a foundational principle of the Christian faith could be so straightforward.

The verse above is easily quoted yet difficult to ascertain. Living by faith is more than a notion. It is not a religious preference or a belief system, neither can it be categorized among other church clichés. True faith will require more of you as an individual. In fact, faith is a systemic process by which you pull in closer to the Lord and listen to the rhythm of his heart for you. Faith is a walk that many begin but few finish. Truthfully, I understand why some may faint prematurely on the road to faith. The devil is just one of many oppositions to your faith. That's right. There is more happening within you than you think. You may be surprised by all that is opposing you. While you may be thinking, *That stupid devil is always in my way,* the devil is not number one on the list of opposers, you are.

To begin in faith, first, you must deal with you. While we would like to believe that faith is automatic, I can assure you it is not. Scripture tells us in Romans 10:17, *"Faith comes by hearing and hearing by the word God."* Hearing is an integral part of your success even after your faith has grown. The word of God is where you start, but faith will carry you to your destiny. Faith in what? Faith in the word of God, faith in the promise of God, and faith in God Himself. Before you can begin this journey, you must first make a decision about what you will believe God for. Decide if what you are believing for is worth fighting for. Your promise will come with a fight, but in faith, you will win every time. If you are willing to stand in faith until your promise manifests, you are ready to begin building your faith. The building process can be tedious at first until you get the hang of it, then it soon becomes a part of you. Know this, your relationship with God the Father is getting ready to go to another level, and if this process works in you the way the Master intends, your relationship with God, the closeness, the oneness, the fellowship you have with Him, will be so overwhelming in your heart, you will cherish this opportunity to walk with Him so closely, the promise will seem to fade in comparison. The thing you have believed for will be a blessing to you and you will praise God for what only He could do. Ultimately, the true blessing is walking with Him step by step.

Your desire for that promise is not as great as the Father's desire to be close to you.

Now is your season to walk with the Father and get to know Him on a deeper level. This road will present some gratifying moments, moments of divine pleasure with God, as well as some opposition but be encouraged. God has a plan to get you from A to Z. Walk it out. See what all He has in store. You'll be surprised by His thoughts about you and His wonderful plan to bring you to an expected end.

God is the Truth

We must first determine that the word of God is the Truth. This entire process hinges on what you believe to be true. Is His word the final truth for your life? Do you believe you can have what He has spoken to you? The word teaches us in Hebrews 11:6, *"But without faith it is impossible to please Him, for he who comes to God must believe that He is a rewarder of those who diligently seek Him."* You have to believe He is a rewarder of those who seek Him. Understand this, things are temporal but God is eternal.

What we seek after must always be God. *Seek ye first the kingdom of God and His righteousness and all these things will be added unto you (Matthew 6:33).* In other words, do not become a stuff chaser. Stuff only lasts temporarily. Strive to become a God chaser and all the other stuff will chase you. Imagine yourself chasing after God with your whole heart. As you chase after Him, you develop a strong sense of attraction like a magnet. While you are chasing God, seeking Him, worshipping Him, you begin to notice blessings are stuck on you. Can you see the peace of God stuck to you, God's favor stuck on you, prosperity sticking to you? Everywhere you go, the blessing of the Lord is attracted to you and finds a place to rest right in your life. That's how it should be in the life of the believer. God's goodness and mercy should chase you down every day of our life. By the end of your faith walk, you will understand it was never about the "stuff"— house, car, promotion, kids, spouse, money, property, or anything. It has always been about God and His unconditional love for you.

God wants you to have exactly what He said you can have. This is an enduring truth I have learned. Remember, He's a father, not just some deep-voice being who shouts from heaven. No, He is with you now and always. He's a good father who absolutely loves each and every one of His children, the obedient ones and the disobedient ones. His love will not change and it hasn't since the beginning of time.

What to Expect When You are Expecting

Often believers find themselves on the journey of faith without truly understanding what to expect when you are expecting from God. It can be discouraging to experience confrontation while standing in faith for your promise. After the initial excitement of walking by faith, it is helpful to know what you might encounter along the way. Keep in mind, you have an adversary that is ready to deter you from receiving. John 10:10 says, "The thief comes only to steal and kill and destroy; I have come that they may have life, and have it to the full." Understand that Jesus is for you living the fullest life possible in spite of the desire of the enemy.

Reputation

The enemy will try to discredit you because he fears your faith in God. Faith, by nature, demands obedience to God. Without obedience, faith would technically be a wish. Faith in God should move you to act in obedience to what He is speaking to you and moving you towards. In James 2:17, we learn that *"faith without works is dead."* Meaning, there must be a corresponding action with my faith. If I say I believe God, then my actions should demonstrate that belief in some fashion. When you step out on faith, be prepared to be the only one willing to take a step of faith. While you may have a few supporters who are willing to cheer you on during your faith walk, realize that only you can take a step of faith for you. On the other hand, you will also encounter those who oppose your decision. Once again, is this faith walk worth fighting for? Will you continue to stand in faith, even if you have to do it alone? I can tell you it is worth fighting for what God said you can have. Never allow naysayers to discourage your decision to trust God. They will talk about you, wrongfully accuse you, and say all manner of things about you, but one thing is certain, you were built to battle on the front lines. Your armor was not made to hide among the bushes, but to stand flat footed with your shield of faith in hand, understanding that no weapon formed against you shall prosper. God said so. The attack on your reputation is a test of faith. Remain focused on your assignment and allow God to deal with your adversary.

Humiliation

Unfortunately, not everyone will understand the "why" behind your faith. Humiliation is a tactic of the enemy designed to make you feel awful and ashamed for believing in God for something big. The enemy will use those around you to make you feel guilty about your faith. Shame and guilt are not from God. God's ways are filled with love and peace. Rest assured, God will allow your enemies to see you prosper in the thing you have believed Him for. So it was for the armies of Israel who were being led into battle by King Saul. For days, Goliath taunted the Israelite army. During this time, he not only intimidated them, he humiliated them by hurling insults at them daily. After hearing the same negativity day in and day out, I imagine the troops were feeling quite discouraged. Even though the Israelites had history with God giving them victory over their enemies, yet and still, humiliation rang in their ears as they stood. However, there was one who was not a part of the army but showed up one day to bring food to his brothers. David, the youngest in his family, had a revelation of the mighty power of God. David took the challenge to defeat this giant and spoke directly to Goliath,

"This day the LORD will deliver you into my hands, and I'll strike you down and cut off your head. This very day I will give the carcasses of the Philistine army to the birds and the wild animals, and the whole world will know that there is a God in Israel" (1 Sam. 17:46).

In essence, David was saying when I kill you, Goliath, and when I overcome the thing which seems impossible, when I do the unthinkable, you will know I belong to the Lord Almighty. You will know that God is with me. You will know it is He who lives in me. Can I encourage you for a moment? The same God that gave little David victory has a plan to bring you victory over all that opposes you in this journey of faith. Just keep walking and you will see it happen.

Restoration

God's plan is to give you exceedingly, abundantly above all that you can ask or even imagine. Whatever you have given up for Him, you will receive it and more. Jesus said, *"Truly I say to you, there is no one who has left house or brothers or sisters or mother or father or children or farms, for My sake and for the gospel's sake, but that he will receive a hundred times as much now in the present age, houses and brothers and sisters and mothers and children and farms, along with persecutions; and in the age to come, eternal life" (Mark 10:29-30).*

The Lord spoke to my husband and I and told us to go back home and start a ministry. We obeyed but did not realize that God's plan was not our plan. We left behind a beautiful home, great paying jobs, a wonderful church family, and the excitement of living in a big city. We desperately wanted to follow after God. However, over the next five years, all of that was put to the test. Praise God for being God. He is all knowing, and His plan is always better than ours. Everything we lost and everything we gave up so this gospel could be preached in our hometown, God multiplied it all back to us. What a blessing. You will recover all that you have lost in this process. You may have lost a loved one in the process, but God will bring joy to your heart again. He will make you glad again. "For the scripture says, "Whoever believes on Him will not be put to shame"" (Romans 10:11). You will never have to worry when your faith is in God.

The Wilderness

Little did I know this simple instruction of moving back home would be the beginning of everything. God wanted to teach me about having faith in Him, not just having a faith, a belief system. Looking back to 2011, I realize that I knew nothing about faith. Even now, I still know very little but God is faithful to allow His Holy Spirit to teach me. In the beginning, there was excitement. Excitement about the unknown. Knowing that God had a plan to be good to us and to prosper us kept our minds dreaming of all the good that was to come. It truly never crossed my mind that there would be what I will reference as a wilderness experience. The wilderness has a purpose and is needful. Its purpose is to:

1. Reveal to you God as your source
2. Cleanse your heart
3. Prepare you for what God has

These three components are essential to the process of faith. You may say, *I am saved and I am pretty sure I know who God is*. Well, let me assure you. There is so much of God, you will never know all there is to know about Him at least in this life. He needs you to truly know Him enough to depend and trust that part of Him. He wants you to know Him as a deliverer, healer, provider, and protector. The greatest place for a believer to be is in a state of dependency upon the Lord. It is when we find ourselves depending on the Lord that we are truly walking by faith. This place is not always comfortable neither does it feel natural. When we feel as if we no longer have control, no clue of what to do, it is there, in that moment, that His great and mighty power is displayed through us.

After the Lord had us move back home, we were homeless with a two year old son and a baby girl on the way. I had no job at the time and, needless to say, life had changed drastically. I became angry with God. Why would He tell me to come home and allow our life to be this hard? Often I gave God my Christian resume hoping he would see things my way and miraculously turn it all around in a day. That did not happen of course. Even more unexpectedly, things seemingly grew worse. We settled into a home that I despised to the point of refusing to put decorations on the walls. I was miserable. The home I left was new and spacious, quietly located in a country like setting with all the amenities of the city. It was perfect! Surprisingly, this was all a part of the Master's plan. During my first three years back, God was doing a major overhaul of my life. Sadly, I thought I was doing well in my walk with God. But I was wrong.

God used this season of my life to reveal God as my source, to cleanse my heart, and to prepare me for what He had planned. I wish I could tell you this was an easy step, but it was rather difficult.

In the wilderness, there is a breaking of dependency on you and what you think you know. Common comforts are removed, and you are left with God as your source. Consider the children of Israel's experience in the wilderness:

"Remember that these forty years the LORD your God led you all the way in the wilderness, so that He might humble you and test you in order to know what was in your heart, whether or not you would keep His commandments. He humbled you, and in your hunger He gave you manna to eat, which neither you nor your fathers had known, so that you might understand that man does not live on bread alone, but on

every word that comes from the mouth of the LORD. Your clothing did not wear out and your feet did not swell during these forty years" (Deuteronomy 8: 2-3).

There are a few key points to see with these verses:

God led them to the wilderness
The wilderness was to humble them
The wilderness was to reveal what was in their hearts
In the wilderness, God would show himself as their source

Walking in the wilderness with God as your guide will lead you to a spiritual examination room and pulls back the layers of your facade to expose the truth about you to you. I find it interesting that God knows the exact condition of our hearts and our faith even though we don't. He knows faith will not work in just any condition, which is why He takes advantage of our wilderness experience to expose the hidden things of our hearts to us. I must warn you, this process can get a little messy in terms of facing your own reality of where you are in God. When all is said and done, our wonderful Father, the master surgeon, will have exposed and removed all those things that have hindered you from going forward in Him. Of course, He needs your willingness to do so. He will only do what you allow Him to do. Be encouraged, you will love the new you.

Renewing Your Mind

Faith is the beginning of all salvation exploits. No one can accept the Lord Jesus apart from using what the Bible says is "the measure of faith." Without this vital component, it is impossible to please the Lord. Then why does it appear to be such a complicated matter? There are various reasons behind why you have or have not seen what you have or have not desired.

When examining your faith, it is important to note that God has not missed it. He is not at fault for any disappointments, let downs, or frustrations you may have experienced. Brace yourself… It's you. Now before we get into the logic behind what you have or have not experienced, please note that this is not meant to be condemning. In no way is God pointing His finger at you in judgment. Never! The bible is clear about our Heavenly Father's position when it comes to His children. Hebrews 12:5-6 says, "And have you completely forgotten this word of encouragement that addresses you as a father addresses his son? It says, "My son, do not make light of the Lord's discipline, and do not lose heart when he rebukes you, because the Lord disciplines the one he loves, and he chastens everyone he accepts as his son."" If you are not certain about anything else in this walk with God, please be certain that He loves you, and He refuses to let you stay in error when He has created you for more.

So what are we doing wrong? More times than not, we are battling with matters of the heart. I'm not particularly speaking in terms of the way we love someone, but in terms of your mind, will, and emotions. In order to shed light on the meaning of this, I need to take a moment to share how man was created.

Man is made up of three dimensions. The most obvious of the three is the body. This is the earth suit we live inside of here on earth. The second dimension is the soul. This is where your mind, will, and emotions operate. Your thinking, your desires, the choices you make and how you feel about them all flow from the soulish realm. The last dimension is your spirit. This is what is born again and totally made new in the moment of salvation (2 Corinthians 5:17). This is the part of you that is 100% like God when you are a born again believer. This is where the leading and prompting of the Lord will happen, not in your mind. In fact, the bible teaches that our natural minds are at enmity with God, for a carnal mind cannot understand the spiritual things of God (Romans 8:7).

The dimension I would like to focus on is the soulish realm. The soulish realm can be a deceitful thing. When you think about how often we make decisions and change our minds based on outside factors and how our emotions switch from one minute to the next, we are in a constant state of change. How can one remain in faith, always ready to contend for the faith, when we have a strong soulish realm that is demanding our thoughts and ultimately dictating our day to day results? Within this realm, we store information from our past experiences, failures and successes, we consider friends and family, opinions of others, and we calculate with reason and intelligence before making a decision. It is interesting how faith does not require any of those things. In fact, to have faith, you need only to believe what God says no matter how outlandish it may seem. Faith is alive and well in your born again spirit. It bypasses your logic and your body and aligns itself with God the Father and His word.

This is a good place to insert that faith hardly ever makes sense. Why? Because God thinks outside the proverbial box and thinks big! It is exciting to know that He has big plans in mind. However, He is looking for your faith to get the job done.

The best and most proven way to tackle your soulish realm is by renewing your mind with the word. Romans 12:2 says **"Do not conform to the pattern of this world, but be transformed by the renewing of your mind. Then you will be able to test and approve what God's will is— his good, pleasing and perfect will."** Transformation is necessary. Many people want the blessings of God in their life but remain unwilling to be transformed. Allowing your mind to change will affect everything in your soulish realm; the way you think, what you believe, how you respond, and what you do.

Now can you understand why your mind must be renewed? It is where we as children of God begin to walk in sync with His will and where we see the greatest manifestations of His glory and love for us. Faith is the catalyst for change. The Lord has given to every man "the measure of faith," however it is up to us to grow that faith. We all have the exact same potential to grow no matter who we are and where we were born, whether we come from a wealthy family or poverty. Your faith will work no matter the circumstances. Faith puts us all on the same playing field.

Patience in Faith

You can have faith for anything that the word of God says you can have. If God said it, then you can have it. When God speaks a word into your life, you can rest in His word being the truth. In Jeremiah 29:11, the Lord declares, "I know the plans I have for you." The word "know" is yada, which means to know with certainty. When He speaks concerning you, He absolutely knows what He is talking about. Allowing this word to permeate your heart and become a part of your life produces faith that will stand the test.

Having faith is only the beginning. You must be willing to hang on to your faith despite opposition. Consider what James, a servant of God and the Lord Jesus Christ has to say, "My brothers, count it all joy when you fall into diverse temptations, knowing that the trying of your faith develops patience. But let patience perfect its work, that you may be perfect and complete, lacking nothing" (James 1:2-4, MEV). On the faith journey you will encounter the temptation to quit, doubt if God really spoke to you, compromise, or even talk yourself out of believing the word. The temptation nor the trial has come for you, but for your faith. Why your faith? It is your faith that pleases God. It is your faith that will move mountains. It is your faith that moves those things that we cannot see to the natural realm where we can see it. I encourage you as the scripture says to count it all joy when these temptations come to try your faith because it is working for you and not against you. Patience is not an easily developed trait. One can only perfect this trait in the midst of something that is testing you. Faith will almost certainly bring you to situations in your life that require you to practice your patience.

I once complained to God that I felt as if He had taken my faith and stretched it out like a rubber band. At any moment, it appeared I would break and lose it all. What I have learned about our Father is He knows what we are capable of, even if we do not know ourselves. Sure enough, my faith endured the test of time and I never popped!

How do we keep our faith from fainting in the day of adversity? Feed it. Feed it daily. How do we feed our faith? We feed our faith by consuming the Word. How do we consume the word? We read it aloud, we meditate on it, we pick it apart, we declare it over ourselves and our situations. When we speak the word, we are in agreement with God and He is in agreement with us. Thus, when you speak, God is speaking at the same time with you. How powerful is that? Do you know what happened when God spoke in Genesis 1? The earth was made! Never allow what you see or do not see to discourage you from speaking. You might feel a little foolish. It may even seem that you are simply lying to yourself. However, that is not the case. You are indeed speaking the truth because you are saying what the Father is saying, and God cannot lie. It is impossible. When we speak, we are in essence, commanding what we see, feel, or think to align itself with the truth that comes from God, and everything has to change!

Faith is a Weapon

Your faith is not only used to bring about the manifestations of the promises of God, faith in the word of God is also a weapon against the attacks of the enemy.

"Be sober and watchful, because your adversary the devil walks around as a roaring lion, seeking whom he may devour. Resist him firmly in the faith, knowing that the same afflictions are experienced by your brotherhood throughout the world" (1Peter 5:8-9).

The word that the Lord gives is also your weapon of choice when the battle arises. Not any word will do. You need to know what the Lord has said and use that against the attacks of the adversary. The devil is seeking after someone he can devour. The scripture also says that he comes with an agenda each time. "The thief cometh not but to steal, kill, and destroy" (John 10:10). That is exactly what he wants to do to your faith— steal it, kill it, and destroy it. However, the Lord has provided the war strategy to overcome the devil's attacks. 1 Peter 5:9 says, "Resist him firmly in the faith." In the Amplified version it reads, "But resist him, be firm in *your* faith [against his attack-rooted, established, immovable]." This is easier said than done. The resisting will come through using your faith. Refuse to move from the place of complete confidence in God.

There will be ample opportunity to walk away. But where is the blessing in that? God wants us to see what He has seen all along. Yet, many of His children back down where the struggle over their faith comes. Like a dog holding on to a rope for a game of tug of war, refuse to let go of your faith. The word of God is the weapon He has given you to fight with, be it a rhema word, which is a right now word spoken to you, or the logos word, which is the written word of God. Ephesians 6:12 says, "For our fight is not against flesh and blood, but against principalities, against powers, against rulers of the darkness of this world, and against spiritual forces of evil in the heavenly places."

How do we fight an invisible opponent? "Therefore take up the whole armor of God that you may be able to resist in the evil day, and having done all, to stand. Stand therefore, having your waist girded with truth, having put on the breastplate of righteousness, having your feet fitted with the readiness of the gospel of peace, *and above all taking the shield of faith, with which you will be able to extinguish all the fiery arrows of the evil one*" (*Ephesians 6: 13-16, MEV*).

We overcome all the fiery darts of the enemy with "the shield of faith." Faith covers you. When doubt, unbelief, or worry race towards you, lift up your faith and your faith will quench, dismantle, snuff out the enemy's ambush against you. Your weaponry is more powerful than what is coming against you when you use your weapon in faith. Be willing to stand and having done all to stand, keep standing!

Overflowing Faith

How will I know when I'm in faith? Real faith doesn't come until an abundance of His word hits. Imagine a cup of water half full. The water is present and you know it. However, there's room for more. So you turn on the tap, place the cup under the faucet, and let it fill to the rim. Yet, there's room for more. So you place the cup back under the running water until finally it happens, overflow! Yes, the cup is completely full and the evidence is that you are now overflowing. Whatever you put in will run out of the cup because there is no more room. Matthew 12:34 says, "out of the *abundance of the heart the mouth speaks.*" It is key to make sure that you are filling up your heart with the word of faith, so when your moment to speak comes, all the scriptures you have poured in will come flooding out of your mouth in faith. One of the problems some believers may experience is finding that their hearts are not full of faith but full of doubt and unbelief. In most cases, they have allowed the challenges they see to infiltrate their hearts with fear and anxiety, better known as a case of the "what-ifs."

You have a right to walk in faith. Faith was given to believers for the sake of God's will being done in the earth. He is working a far greater good through our lives because of faith and has guaranteed the completion of this good work until the day of Jesus Christ.

God knew before we ever stepped on the scene, that we would be an imperfect people, and yet He trusted us with something so amazing and powerful that when we enter into the faith arena, we would then become perfect towards God. The Lord sincerely desires for us to know who we are and whose we are.

God wants you to have His overflowing faith so that you can do what He does. God used faith even in the beginning of creation. In Genesis, when the Lord says, "Let there be…," I am certain He believed that what He said would happen. God has never questioned whether He would be able to accomplish any given task. No, the Lord is certain, fully convinced, persuaded by what he speaks. Second Corinthians 4:13-14 says, "We have the same spirit of faith. As it is written, "I believed and therefore I have spoken."" When your faith is overflowing, you can speak like God speaks. You can decree a thing and it shall be so.

Our challenge in seeing what God said is not saying what we see but rather learning to say what He says.

"Be attentive, brothers lest there be in any of you an evil, unbelieving heart, and you depart from the living God" (Hebrews 3:12).

Notice here, an unbelieving heart is being called evil.

"For who were those who heard and rebelled? Was it not all of those who came out of Egypt led by Moses? And with whom was He provoked for forty years? Was it not with those who had sinned, whose bodies fell in the wilderness? And to whom did He swear that they would not enter His rest, but to those who were disobedient? So we see that they were unable to enter because of unbelief" (Hebrews 3:16-19, ESV).

God promised Abraham and his descendants the land of Canaan, a land flowing with milk and honey. This land was handpicked by God to be a blessing to the children of Israel. He delivered them from years of slavery, caused their enemies to be defeated, parted the Red Sea so they could cross over on dry land, fed them with manna and quail on the way to the promise land, turned the bitter waters of Marah into sweet water so they could have drink, sustained their clothing and shoes during their travel through the wilderness, and caused them to remain healthy so that there would be no feeble among them. I would say God was serious about them possessing the land He had promised to their forefather Abraham. However, when they saw giants in the land, their faith was shattered and they fell into doubt and unbelief. They refused the blessing of God and let go of their faith. Unfortunately, that particular generation missed what God wanted them to have and died in the wilderness.

Our Father has many wonderful promises for His children. There are blessings that He has desired to give us simply because He loves us. The Lord, in his mercy, reveals His thoughts and plans to us so we know what He has already planned for us. Everyone loves to hear the good things God has planned, but we must carry the faith to bring those things into the now.

Take Time to Build

Faith comes by hearing and hearing by the word of God. This implies that it comes but there should be a continual "coming" of faith by a continual "hearing of faith." Faith is not microwavable, popping into your heart in a matter of minutes. In some cases, faith seems to flow quicker than in others. There are those seasons where you will need to build your faith so that it can overflow. Faith is to be spoken out of your mouth. When words of faith flow, things begin to change.

In my time of ministry, I have counseled many individuals who feel as if their faith isn't working. They make claims, of which I am sure they do, of speaking the word and confessing the word over their circumstances to seemingly no avail. What they really mean is, *I'm doing all the necessary outward actions and I can't see the difference yet.* This is a very real statement. However, I try to encourage them to keep building their faith by hearing the word because the moment will come when faith fills their hearts and will begin to overflow out of them effortlessly. They will have transformed their thinking and speaking in what appears to be a moment.

Faith takes time to build. We should always be working on building our faith, not just in the moments when we feel we truly need it the most. Overflowing faith is achievable with a disciplined lifestyle of hearing the word, agreeing with the word, and speaking the word.

Faith will be overflowing when you begin to speak faith first. I'm not talking about quoting scripture with no revelation of it in your life. I'm speaking in terms of you responding in faith. In those moments where fear begins to threaten your health, marriage, finances, or family, you can, instead of agreeing with fear and assuming the worst scenario, simply refuse to succumb to the pressure of the enemy and begin to release words of faith over yourself.

Faith is an extender that provides a connection point for the Lord to legally move in our lives. Wait! Legally? Yes, our faith gives God permission to work freely in our lives in accordance to His will for us. Without this faith, everything falls on us. By divine design, the Lord orchestrated spiritual laws that He Himself would not violate. Rather, He chose to provide Holy Spirit to reveal Jesus (the word made flesh) to His children so that we might know and understand the perfect will of God.

There may be times where what we see appears to be opposite of what God said. Nonetheless, that is why we are called believers. We believe. We are the ones who hope against hope; we believe with no reason to believe other than the simple truth of, "God said so." I encourage you to be open to all that our heavenly Father is saying concerning you. He is looking to show Himself strong on your behalf. Mixing what God has spoken with faith will be the greatest combination of power working in your life.

Respond in Faith

Developing overflowing faith is key when pressing times are among us. It is critical to learn to respond to adversity first with our faith. It goes without saying, this is easier said than done. However, our first response can determine the outcomes of our situation. This was certainly the case for a mother found in 2 Kings 4:22-26.

This Shunammite woman was blessed with a son by the prophet Elisha. One day, the child was working in the fields with his father and fell ill. The father sent him to his mother, and by evening he died on his mother's lap. She did not give in to this pressure. She was given this child as a result of her continuous generosity to the man of God. This mother arose and placed her dead son on the bed upstairs and quickly began preparations to go find the prophet who first told her she would conceive.

"Then she called to her husband and said, "Please send me one of the servants and one of the donkeys, that I may run to the man of God and return." He said, "Why will you go to him today? It is neither new moon nor sabbath." And she said, "*It will be* well." Then she saddled a donkey and said to her servant, "Drive and go forward; do not slow down the pace for me unless I tell you." So she went and came to the man of God at Mount Carmel.

When the man of God saw her at a distance, he said to Gehazi his servant, "Behold, there is the Shunammite. Please run now to meet her and say to her, 'Is it well with you? Is it well with your husband? Is it well with the child?'" And she answered, "It is well."

Notice, as she called for a servant to drive her to the man of God, her husband calls to her and asks, "Is everything okay?" Her response is shocking and yet full of faith. One would think she is lying to protect the family from such a tragic moment, but she is now in the moment where her response is everything. Upon her arrival to meet with the prophet Elisha, Gehazi presented yet another opportunity to respond based on her natural circumstances. You would have expected her to respond hysterically at the loss of her child. On the contrary, she doesn't respond in this manner at all. In fact, the writer does not even indicate as to whether she had tears in her eyes. We do know that her haste aroused suspicion from her husband, but no other signs of distress were given. Without pause, she responds again, "All is well," and continues on her journey. She was totally convinced that when she found this prophet, all would be well. Her son would live because of the God of this prophet. She had faith that His God would bring her son back to life. And He did!

Having faith in God is no guarantee that everything will work just the way you've planned with no hiccups along the way. We have to be okay with knowing God can handle the hiccups too. Trust is a must in this walk with Him. Begin training yourself to trust God in the small things in your life so when challenges arise, you will respond in faith.

Start believing God to help you find your keys. Instead of panicking about being late for work, respond in faith and say, "Father, you know where my keys are and I thank you for leading me to them quickly, in Jesus name." Faith is not restricted to those insanely high mountains we sometimes have to face. Our faith is for everyday use. God loves for us to believe in Him to meet our needs and help us with our day to day challenges. No matter how small or insignificant something seems to be, try

God first. Most believers use their faith as a last resort. I strongly believe that many moments of frustration could be avoided if we would learn to respond in faith first.

Manna for the Moment

God does not only use your faith to acquire promises given, but He will also use your faith to bring out the best in you. When God called for my husband and I to head back home to start a ministry, I was less than enthused about the assignment. Moving home was not in my plans. However, I knew this pull was from the Lord and I could not refuse. So we made plans to obey.

I believed that through obedience to what the Lord had spoken to us, transitioning would be smooth sailing. I expected new jobs to open up like the Red Sea, to find a beautiful new home filled with good things. Needless to say, I was wrong. Very wrong. The many obstacles we faced in the beginning were enough to send us back to the big city with our tails between our legs. It was rough. I remember living in a home that felt three times smaller than the one we moved from, with two kids now and enough furniture to furnish a new four bedroom home. Unfortunately, misery was my company for many days and I began to resent God. How could He call us to this city under these conditions? *Life was better where we were*, I thought. I found myself complaining about the circumstances, much like the Israelites, even though God had clearly provided manna.

Even through the dire circumstances we faced, God still provided. God gave manna.

It is imperative to understand that the manna God gives is only for the moment. It is not a place of permanency. It is only present to meet your current need. This manna is not intended for long term use, but rather a means of supply by the Father to see you through. Recognizing what is assigned to you as manna is key in maintaining laser focus in faith. Manna is typically not what you expected but it does meet the need. It can be disguised in many forms — unexpected checks in the mail, favor with people, or maybe God will cause what you do have to stretch a lot further than you expected. The house God had for us was not what I expected, but it did meet the need. The way God gave me my new job was not at all what I had planned, and yet He was able to bring it to pass.

In the wilderness, the children of Israel were not happy campers simply because they no longer possessed the luxury of having control over what they ate. You can avoid this trap of falling into being unappreciative like they did by discerning what God has placed before you to meet your need and being thankful that He is a need meeter. I fell into the trap of ungratefulness which led to bitterness in serving God. I knew God had not called us to live in a place of struggle or in a place where we could not meet our own needs. Seemingly, our independence had taken a turn and left us feeling blind as to what was next for us.

Could it be that maybe God did plan for our faith in His word to lead us right into a place of destiny and dependence upon Him? Blind faith is a real walk with God. There's no such thing as looking ahead or peeping to see what's coming next, because you have no clue what God is up to. Quite often, He only reveals enough for your obedience. The rest is walking and trusting that He is indeed a good Father and His plans for you are good. Accepting the manna means you are grateful. This opens the door for greater abundance in your life. Be thankful for His manna, His glorious provision.

Provision is Always Now

"But my God shall supply all your need according to his riches in glory by Christ Jesus" (Philippians 4:19, KJV).

The Lord has made it clear that He is the supplier of all of our needs. Not only is He the supplier, but He has also supplied through what He has (his riches) in glory. The Lord has made all things available through Christ Jesus. The scripture does not reference what good works we must perform or what we must already have in possession to obtain such a wonderful supply from Him. Rather, He discloses the truth of all of our needs being supplied based on His riches through Christ Jesus.

As a child of God, I struggled with this concept. I knew the scripture but failed to understand what it really meant in the life of a believer. As far back as I can remember, I have always had a need, typically a financial one. Like many people, I prayed for money. As I grew in the Lord, I prayed for increase. That sounded like a more sophisticated Christian word to use, and yet the result was still the same. I only wanted more money. The truth is I didn't need more money, I needed God's wisdom. But who wants to pray for wisdom when they have bills pilling up and are in need of food. Oddly enough, this is when I learned one of the most valuable lessons about receiving the provisions of God by faith.

Shortly after my daughter was born, we were swamped with medical bills. One day, while driving to work, I remember praying, asking God to increase us even more. I heard these words, "Provision is always now." In that moment, the Lord began to teach me the difference between storehouse blessings and provision. "Lord what do you mean provision is always now?" I asked. He explained to me provision will be there when you need it. I soon realized I had been asking for storehouse blessings, those blessings that sit in our possession awaiting a need. I was wanting God to bless us with so much money we could completely come out of debt instantly and never worry about money again. Let me insert. Yes, God will bless you in that manner. For me, He was using that moment of my faith to show me Him as a Father and my supplier.

This concept is similar to a football play. When the quarterback throws the ball down field, it isn't intended to touch anyone's hands until it reaches the person designated to catch it. The receiver knows how far to run, what direction he needs to run towards, and he knows when to extend his arms to reach out and capture the ball. So it is with the Lord's provision. We listen to Him to know the details of obtaining what He has provided. At the right moment, you will run right into your provision. He knows what you need and when you need it. Your faith will bring you into that divine moment so that you can receive your supply.

Your faith will bring not only this provision into your life but you will soon begin to experience the abundance He has for you. Ask yourself, "Am I believing God for His supply, or am I believing for God to make me rich so I don't have to worry?" Unfortunately, I wanted the latter. I have learned since, and you will also, that it is not about what you need, it's who you need. Grasping the understanding of what Jesus has already done on the cross automatically places the children of God in position of all needs met, whether we can see it or not. My needs were met. Years later, I reflect back to those moments of despair and discouragement and realize that Jesus had already provided through His sacrifice for us. That is the promise of Philippians 4:13. By Jesus, because of Jesus, we are supplied. So our faith is not to be used to convince God to meet our needs, it is used to receive what He has provided through Christ Jesus. When you need the provision of God, grab it with your faith.

When praying for provision, keep in mind, whatever you are in need of is readily available upon request. Think of it this way, God's provision is similar to that of a convenience store. When you walk in, things are prepared and ready to be purchased. In typical circumstances, no one has to go prepare your bag of chips or candy. You simply pick up what you need, purchase it, and go. Whatever you need, simply ask in faith, receive by faith, and say thank you by faith.

"And whatsoever ye shall ask in my name, that will I do, that the Father may be glorified in the Son. If ye shall ask any thing in my name, I will do it" (John 14:13-14). Asking for the will of God is always a yes. Ask in the name of Jesus, and He will do it.

Growing your Faith

Let's examine two verses of scripture to determine how we are to grow our faith:

"So then faith cometh by hearing, and hearing by the word of God" (Romans 10:17, KJV).

"For I say, through the grace given unto me, to every man that is among you, not to think of himself more highly than he ought to think; but to think soberly, according as God hath dealt to every man the measure of faith" (Romans 12:3, KJV).

Romans 10:17 tells us how faith comes to us and Romans 12:3 explains where faith comes from. Faith has been given to believers to receive from God all that He has promised and made available through His Son Jesus Christ.

God has given us the responsibility of taking *the measure of faith* He has given to us and to continually grow this faith. We all have this faith. However, the growth process is up to us. How can I grow my faith? It comes by hearing the word of God. Not just by hearing random words or sermons, but rather, a specific word for the specific areas we are needing to use our faith. This is a good moment to insert that it is better to have a focal point when you begin to grow your faith. I have learned that it is extremely overwhelming to grow my faith for every possible thing I may need or may face in life, so start small.

Growing your faith should not be a burden to you. It should cause you to draw closer to God as you hear His word concerning your life. Faith in its infant stage begins with hope. Hope is the road that leads to faith. The Bible says in Hebrews 11:1, "Now faith is the substance of things hoped for and the evidence of things not seen." Hope is not faith but rather it is the substance. When that substance is built in your heart, it produces faith. Faith is the complete assurance that what God has spoken is the Truth. Faith comes when an abundance of the word hits. Faith floods out of our hearts and flows out of our mouth without hesitation. You will know faith is fully developed when you are completely sure that what the Word says is so.

How do I grow my faith? Where should I begin?
Use these steps and begin implementing them into your daily routine:

Find what the word says concerning your specific situation.
Begin speaking (out loud) the word over your life every day, multiple times a day. Train yourself to speak the word only concerning your situation.
Meditate on that word, mull it over in your mind, allow Holy Spirit to reveal more and more about that word to you.
Begin to give praise to the Lord for what He has done in your life.

Growing faith takes time and consistency. This may seem challenging, but God is helping you every step of the way. You are not alone. The Lord desires to see His word at work in you. The word says in Isaiah 55:11, "So shall my word be that goeth forth out of my mouth: it shall not return unto me void, but it shall accomplish that which I please, and it shall prosper in the thing whereto I sent it." God is watching over the very word you are using to make certain that it prospers in your life.

What Do You See

As you grow your faith, you should be able to see spiritually, your end result. Vision is critical when walking by faith. Not the vision of our natural circumstances. I'm referring to the vision of the spirit that causes you to be able to see what God sees concerning you. This type of vision is also known as your imagination. Yes, God will use your imagination as a tool to get you to your destiny. The first place imagination is used in scripture is in Genesis 11:4-6:

"And they said, Go to, let us build us a city and a tower, whose top may reach unto heaven; and let us make us a name, lest we be scattered abroad upon the face of the whole earth. And the Lord came down to see the city and the tower, which the children of men builded. And the Lord said, Behold, the people is one, and they have all one language; and this they begin to do: and *now nothing will be restrained from them, which they have imagined to do.*"

The mission was clear, to build a city and a tower that would reach to heaven. The people had a plan and purposed so strongly in their hearts that a vision was birthed within them and now nothing would be restrained from them, which they had imagined to do. They could all see the big picture.

What have you imagined to do? What can you see through the lens of faith? Developing vision takes time alone with God. You may not be able to see instantly as you are growing your faith, but vision will come. In fact, God wants you to see what He sees. Why? Because it empowers your faith like fuel on a fire. It gives a boost to your walk and helps you to stand strong in the day of adversity. Vision for your life should come from the one who came to give you life and that more abundantly. There is a life that Jesus has in mind for you and it is full of abundance. Take some time to sit with God and allow Him to reveal His vision. Creating a vision board with those images of what He has shown you will help to keep you focused in your faith.

"And the Lord answered me, and said, Write the vision, and make it plain upon tables, that he may run that readeth it. For the vision is yet for an appointed time, but at the end it shall speak, and not lie: though it tarry, wait for it; because it will surely come, it will not tarry" (Habakkuk 2:2-3).

Even though this vision is for an appointed time, it will surely come to pass.

The enemy will often use your natural vision and the power of suggestion to cause you to create an image in your mind. After we have meditated on the suggestion offered by satan, we find ourselves seeing the manifestations of what we have seen happen in our minds over and over. Typically, his suggestions are rooted in fear and always lead to sin and unbelief in God's word.

Our imagination is a powerful tool in seeing the manifestations of God's promises in our life. We possess the ability right now to see ourselves healthy, full of joy, free from addictions, and walking in peace. God's view of you is glorious. He knows what you shall be. He wants to show you what you are becoming in Christ. Despite the opposite view of your current reality, I encourage you to lean in to God's heart concerning you and listen to what He says. Allow His words to deem you worthy of the vision He is speaking and birth a holy vision of your destiny. Our Father sees the end from the beginning. Our lives lay open before him and He's working in us through our faith being yielded, willing surrender to see what He sees and accept what He says as our final truth.

There is something so powerful that opens within the children of God when we realize who we are and where we are going. We begin to operate in such clarity and move in this beautiful flow of Holy Spirit. This is truly when we can boldly declare, "and nothing shall be restrained from me that I have imagined to do."

Laser-Focused Faith

Determining what to believe for is paramount in this process. I'm sure many of us can find areas in our life in which we could use a boost of faith. There are other areas where we may feel like we've got everything under control. While it is possible to use your faith in all areas of your life, and you should, there will arise situations and circumstances that will demand laser-focused faith. Laser-focused by definition simply means to pinpoint or to intensely pay attention to something or someone specific. Acquiring laser focus with your faith will take discipline and time. It is helpful to understand that time can build unnecessary pressure if your focus begins to shift from what God can do to what you can do.

God the Father does not operate in time, but rather uses time to work for your good. Consider the story of Lazarus found in John 11. Jesus knew that his friend Lazarus was sick and at the point of death. He was urged to come and see about him. Surprisingly, Jesus remained two more days at a neighboring city. When Jesus finally arrived at Bethany where Lazarus was, he had already been in the tomb four days. And yet, when Jesus called for him to come out of the tomb, Lazarus did.

Time does not move God. It obeys God. Don't allow your faith to feel the pressures of time sensitive issues. Laser focused faith remains at rest while God does the work. The pressure does not belong to you, it belongs to God.

Begin developing this focus by pinpointing what you are believing for God to do. This can happen several ways. No matter what way is chosen, it should be connected to God's will for your life. The Lord may ask you to choose what you want so He can bless you.

I remember when my husband and I were searching for a new home. We had outgrown our current home quickly and needed space to accommodate our needs. When we met with our realtor and began the search, the outlook was not promising. The house we wanted was not available and all the other homes we looked at over the course of three years were not right for us. We even attempted to settle for something we didn't love but could never bring ourselves to commit. When it seemed hopeless, we started tossing around the idea of building a house. This was not our heart's desire, especial in the busy season of life we were in. There was no time to work out all the details of building a home from the ground up. Finally, one Wednesday night after church, the Lord asked me a question that I will never forget. He said, "Ask me for what you will and I will do it." In that moment, I knew God wanted us to make up our minds to believe Him for one way or the other, but to definitely be specific so He could bring it to pass in our lives. That night we decided on buying a specific home. In a matter of a few months, the house we wanted came on the market and the rest is history.

Your faith needs a direct object. Your faith needs you to believe for something. If your faith had hands what would it grab off of God's shelf of provision? If you want to be healed, what specifically needs to be healed? Maybe you do not have a diagnosis, but you do know you want the pain to be removed from your body and be able to do what you have not been able to do for years. Be specific, be laser focused in your faith.

Many times people ask me to pray for them. When I ask what do they want me to pray about, they say, "just everything." While I completely know what they mean, this statement does not allow me to attach my faith to anything in particular. If you are not believing for anything in particular, that is exactly what you will get, nothing in particular.

It is not offensive to the Lord that you ask for specific blessings. Where we cross the line most often is when we tell God to make things happen this way or that. Our heavenly Father does not need your strategies or methodologies to get you what you have desired of Him. He needs your faith. If God ever had a need, and truly He doesn't in the sense like you and I have needs to be sustained in life, it would be our faith on the earth. Luke 18:8 says, "*Nevertheless when the Son of man cometh, shall he find faith on the earth?*"

You may know exactly what you are believing for. Maybe it is your heart's desire to have a job that you enjoy, one that provides a better salary, flexible hours, with a shorter drive than what you currently drive each morning. While this is not a life or death situation or a need, it may be a desire of your heart and the approach is the same. Go to the Lord and ask him for your desire. Ask Him for a word to stand on while He brings this to pass in your life. With the word He gives, remain laser focused. You may be presented with other opportunities that may partially meet your desires. Follow the peace of God. You can discern if there is peace in taking the opportunity. If not, be still and wait on the Lord. He is always working behind the scenes to bless you.

Keep in mind, satan loves to bring distractions and things that shimmer and glitter to make you feel like this is a God thing that you cannot walk away from. Second Corinthians 5:7 tells us that we are to walk by faith and not by sight. Faith does not look at the natural neither considers what the circumstances are, but rather yields itself to God's truth and God's way. This can only be spiritually felt by following the peace of God in your heart. Holy Spirit will prompt you in making the right decision. Obey His leading.

Friends, God is love. He loves us like a Father and He will not stop loving us. God had something so much better waiting for us. The house God had in mind was the house I desired. Trust in God's plan. His plan is perfect and without flaw. I've learned over time that whatever He does for us, it's always for our good.

Jesus says to his disciples in John 14:10, "Do you not believe that I am in the Father, and the Father in Me? The words that I speak to you I do not speak on My own authority; but the Father who dwells in Me does the works." As you bring your faith into focus, keep in mind, your job is to believe, speak His word only, and the Lord will bring it to pass.

God is Thinking About You

Faith is indeed a necessity of life and godliness. Nevertheless, your faith is not the most important thing to God. You are. Be aware of the times you begin to be overwhelmed by feelings of stress, anxiousness, frustration, or discouragement while standing in faith for the promises of God. One of the greatest comforts of being His child is knowing that you are always on His mind and that He cares about you more than you care about the thing you are believing for. Regardless of where you are in this journey, continually remind yourself of God's unfailing love for you not things.

Sitting at my kitchen table perplexed about how long my breakthrough was taking, I sat calculating all of my great faith accomplishments and making certain that I had done all of the right things to yield the desired results. The more I pondered the process, the more disheartened I felt. Then I heard the Lord say, "I'm more concerned about you than that." Embedded in those words, I could sense the Lord's heart for me.

The Lord has already determined what to do about the issues of life.

Romans 8:28 explains that all things work together for the good of those who love Him and are called according to His purpose. The phrase, "work together," comes from the Greek word synergei (soon-erg-eh'-o), which is where we get our English word synergy. This word implies that God takes all of the different pieces of our life, the good with the bad, and is able to draw them together like a magnet to metal, forming something greater and more powerful for His divine purpose. We have no need to fret when challenged in our faith. We can be bold and walk in the greatest assurance when we know who we are and whose we are.

It is wise to keep first things first. The word teaches us that there are blessings that flow naturally as a result of seeking first things first. Matthew 6:33 says, "But seek ye first the kingdom of God, and His righteousness; and all these things shall be added unto you" (KJV). When we pursue the kingdom of God and His righteousness, everything else will pursue us. We, who are God chasers, are being chased by the glorious things He has prepared for us.

Give God Your Desires

In this quest of faith, we will come to know certain aspects of the journey as common place. We will come to expect the adversity, no matter how unwanted it may be. We will even find ourselves becoming more strategic with our faith for the things of God. Even in all of that, we must be mindful to not allow our relationship with the Father to dwindle to second place in our life. There may be a moment in time where you begin to focus all of your attention on attaining a goal or desire. Unbeknownst to you, you quickly lose sight of walking in fellowship with God and communing with Him.

Our heavenly Father is seeking such a relationship with you and desires to spend time with you. As His children, we must remain focused on our Father and what we can do to serve Him. This requires humility, patience and a great level of trust.

I'm reminded of my early days in college when I first began to seek the Lord personally. I remember wanting to join a sorority, however, there were some things that I needed to ensure prior to my acceptance into the process of becoming a member of this sisterhood. Late one afternoon, I received a phone call from the chapter president stating their interest in having me become a part of their sorority, but she was uncertain about a few things and needed to confirm whether or not I would be able to do this. She told me she was going to make a phone call and would let me know as soon as she knew an answer. I hung up the phone and immediately got on my knees to pray. I told the Lord that I really wanted to be a part of the sorority like many others in my family. I then prayed something that shocked me as I heard it come out of my mouth for the first time. I said, "Lord, if you let me join this sorority, I'll serve you, and if you don't let me join, I'm still going to serve you." Almost immediately after saying this prayer, my phone rang with a yes.

I meant every word of that prayer. For the first time, I realized God was more important to me that getting what I wanted. I sincerely believe when we give our desires to the Lord and allow Him to do what He desires to do with them, then we can walk in the overflowing abundance of desires fulfilled. Over time, I've come to understand that many of our desires have been given to us by the Lord. For the first time, I had a new revelation of the scripture found in Psalm 37:4,

"Delight thyself also in the Lord: and *he shall give thee the desires of thine heart.*" God gave me the desire to be a part of a sorority, and He used me greatly within it to share Christ with others.

One of the hesitations of giving your desires to God is that we may feel like God won't do it the way we think, or maybe it will take forever for God to do it. Maybe we feel that God might just say no concerning what we desire. Please understand that not every desire you have is from the Lord. Some desires stem from the lust of the eye, the lust of the flesh, and the pride of life. One way to know if it is a God desire is to give it back to Him. Entrust the Lord with bringing it pass. Provide your faith in what He can do for you and through you. If your desire is something you cannot place in His care, you probably don't need that desire.

Having a relationship with the Lord is not a Sunday morning or Wednesday night type of relationship. Only seeking the Lord when you need Him to do something is no way to maintain a healthy connection between you and your creator. While we are developing faith in Almighty God, it goes without saying, that you are also building and establishing a personal relationship with Him as well. What good is faith without love?

"For in Jesus Christ neither circumcision availeth anything, nor uncircumcision; but faith which worketh by love" (Galatians 5:6). Love makes our faith work. Not only should we walk in love towards others, but we also must walk in love with God. He desires to be close to you. There's so much to know about the Lord that we will spend a lifetime just scratching the surface of knowing Him.

More Than a Journey

"Yes indeed, it won't be long now." God's Decree.

"Things are going to happen so fast your head will swim, one thing fast on the heels of the other. You won't be able to keep up. Everything will be happening at once—and everywhere you look, blessings! Blessings like wine pouring off the mountains and hills. I'll make everything right again for my people Israel:" (Amos 9:13-14, MSG).

The day is quickly approaching where you will begin to see the manifestation of what you are believing for. Seemingly, those things that took a lifetime to come will come. Many are discouraged well before manifestation arrives, but those who wait for it will have their joy made full. Manifestations are not just about receiving in the natural. My prayer is that you will come to know that the blessing was in the journey. Learning all those little lessons along the way, feeling closer to God than ever before, realizing just how much the Father loves you is so much greater than the "thing." Quick and unexpected blessings are wonderful, but there is a deeper level of blessing that flows from the Father's heart to those who are willing to wait on Him. Consider this verse of scripture:

"The Lord is not slow to fulfill His promise as some understand slowness, but is patient with you, not wanting anyone to perish but everyone to come to repentance" (2 Peter 3:9).

Notice the phrase, "but is patient with you." Often we feel that the work of patience is all on us as the believer. We are generally told to wait upon the Lord as if God needs more time to perform a miracle in our lives. On the contrary, it is the Lord who is patient with us in this process. He awaits the development of our faith and rejoices as He witnesses firsthand the transformations of His dear children. As much as we would like for the blessings to come immediately, we must evaluate the need for the journey. What might we forfeit in our lives if we abort the journey simply because we have succumb to the pressures of time?

God is the creator of time. He himself is not bound by time. Time does not dictate when God should or should not do anything, but as a matter of choice, the Lord utilizes time skillfully as an instrument to bring about His own glory in our lives. Could it be perhaps, that the Father agrees with our faith and is continually working behind the scenes of our life, all the while developing us to be in the right place, at the right time, with the right heart, to receive?

The journey of faith is designed to bring about the you God has always had in mind. Growth is a natural part of life, but it is intentional in the spirit. Longevity in the faith does not equate to growth over time. But rather it is when we make the conscious decision to allow our Father to grow us in every area of our life. The faith walk is more than a journey, it is a perpetual discovery of God's enduring love for you through His will and His way.

www.ingramcontent.com/pod-product-compliance
Lightning Source LLC
Chambersburg PA
CBHW022000290426
44108CB00012B/1147